A Is for Animals!

THIS BOOK BELONGS TO

For general information on our other products and services or to obtain technical support, please contact our Customer Care Department within the U.S. at (866) 744-2665, or outside the U.S. at (510) 253-0500.

Rockridge Press publishes its books in a variety of electronic and print formats. Some content that appears in print may not be available in electronic books, and vice versa.

Interior Designer: Liz Cosgrove
Cover Designer: Liz Cosgrove
Photo Art Director: Michael Hardgrove
Editors: Jeanine Le Ny and Kristen Depken
Production Editor: Ashley Polikoff
Illustrations © Robin Boyer and Terry Marks, 2019
Author photograph courtesy Jamie Healy

ISBN: 978-1-64152-786-6

A
Is for Animals!

Preschool COLORING Book

Rachael Smith

ROCKRIDGE
PRESS

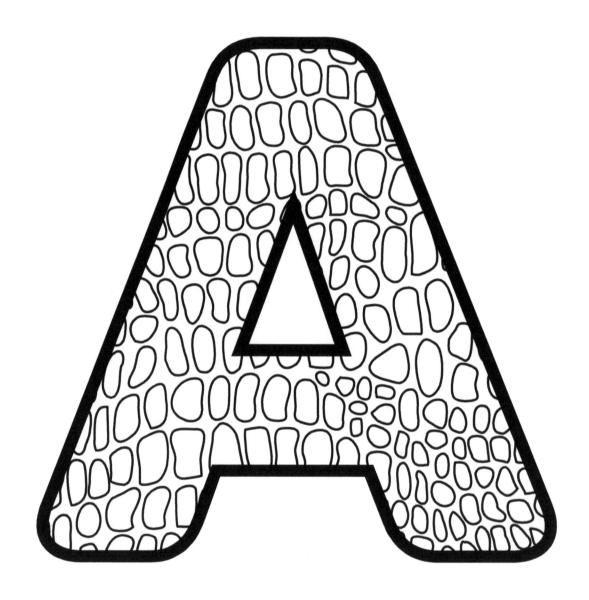

Alligator

Alligators have up to 80 sharp teeth!

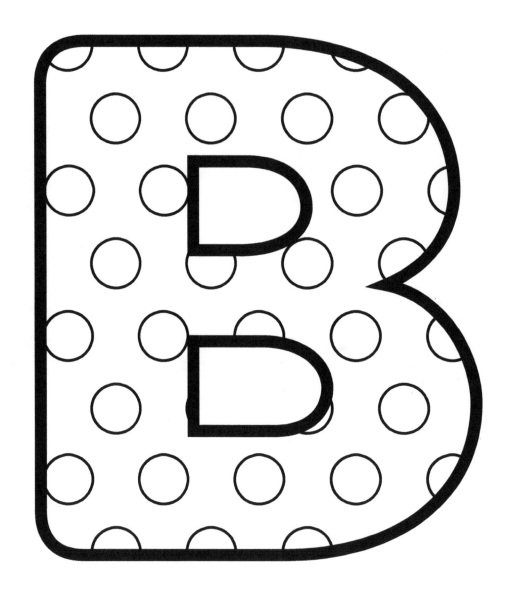

Bear

Bears are great swimmers.

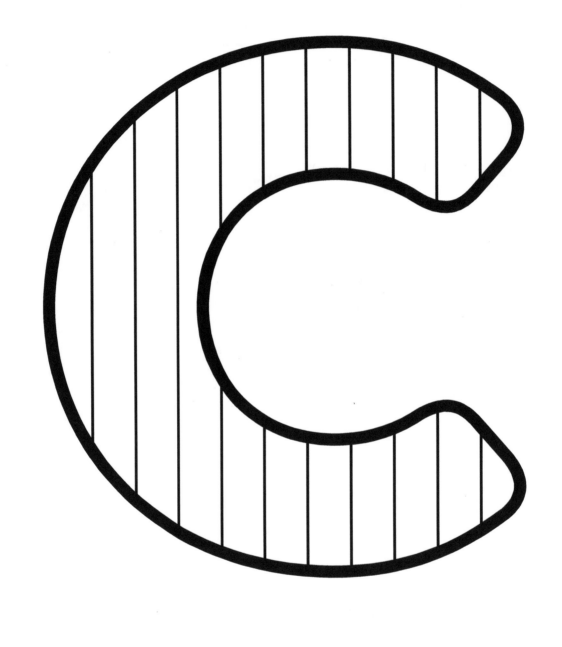

Cat

Cats love to sleep.

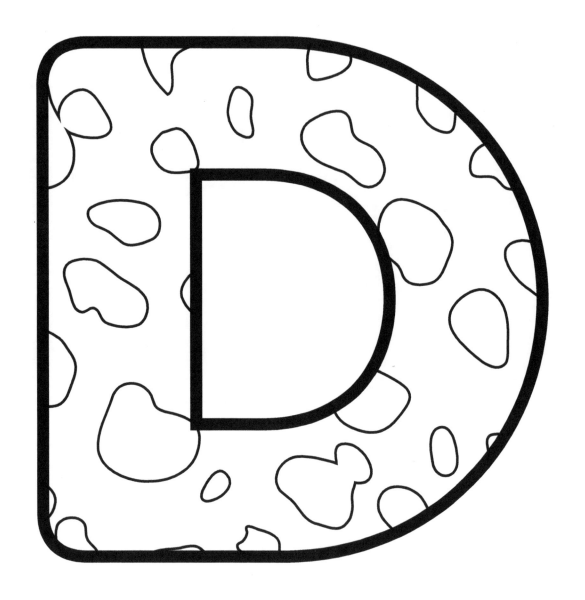

Dog

Every dog's noseprint is unique,
just like a human fingerprint.

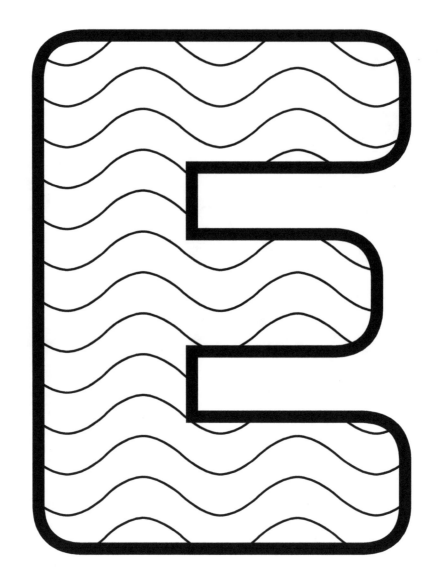

Elephant

Of all the animals that live on land,
elephants are the largest!

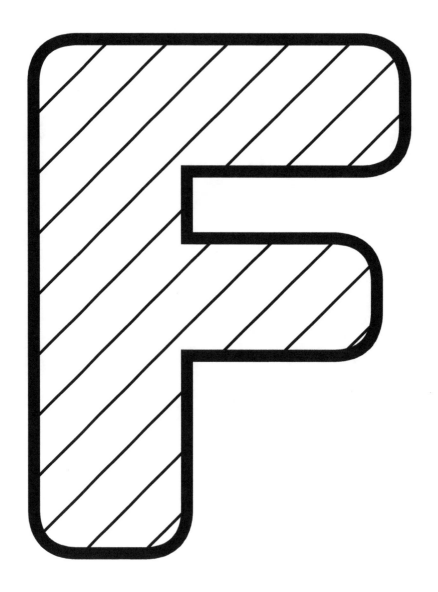

Fox

Foxes dig dens to protect
their babies, or kits.

Giraffe

Giraffes use their long necks to reach for leaves to snack on high in the treetops.

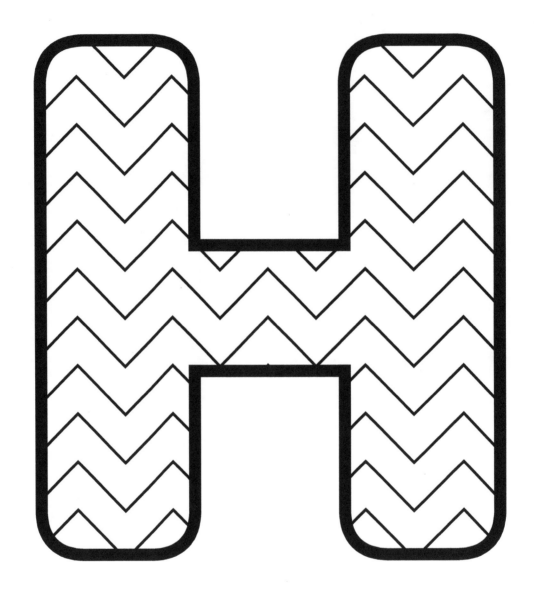

Hamster

Hamsters carry food by stuffing it into pouches in their cheeks.

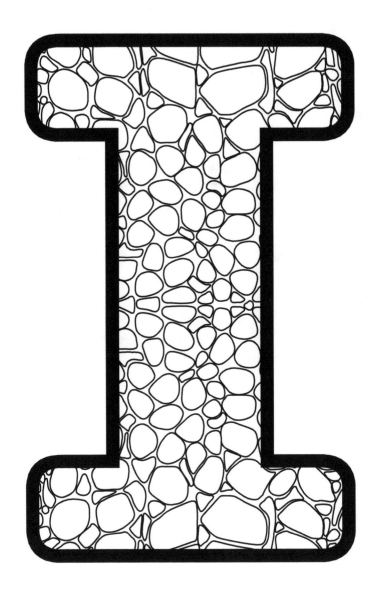

Iguana

Iguanas relax in the sun to stay warm.

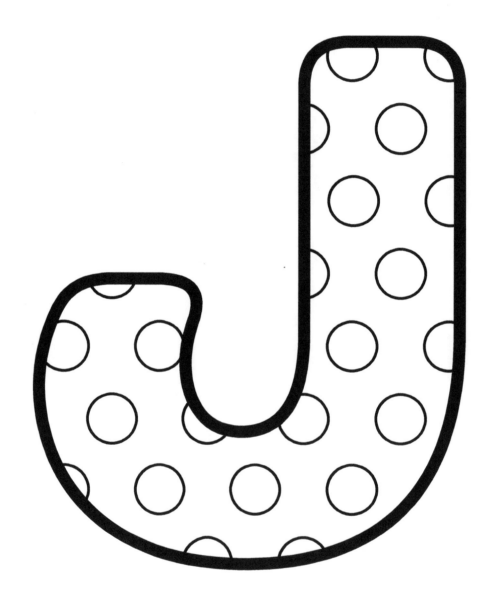

Jellyfish

Jellyfish use their tentacles
to stun their prey.

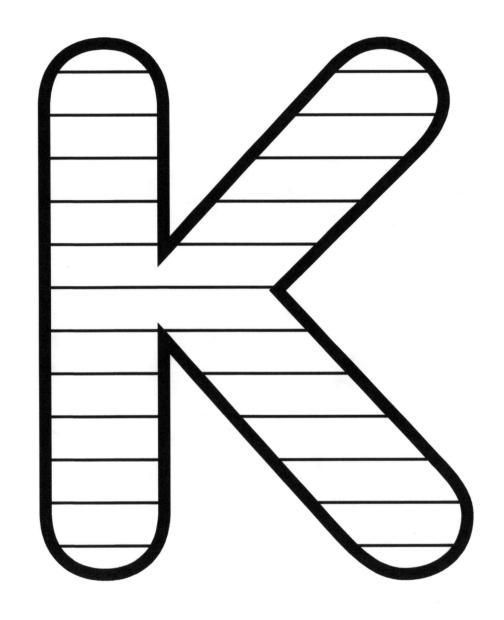

Koala

A newborn koala is called a joey.
It's only the size of a jelly bean!

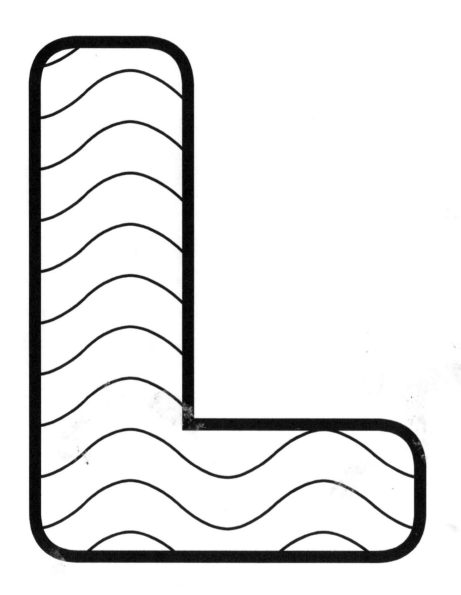

Lion

Lions live in groups called prides.

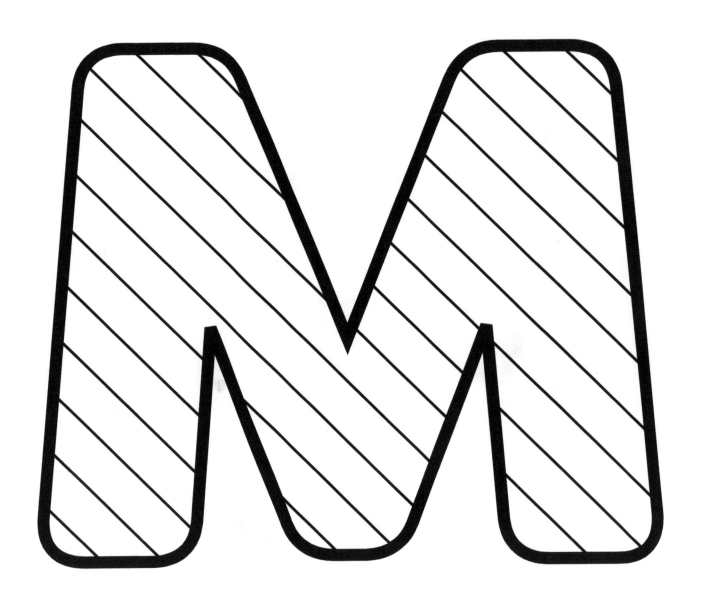

Monkey

Monkeys are super smart and very curious.

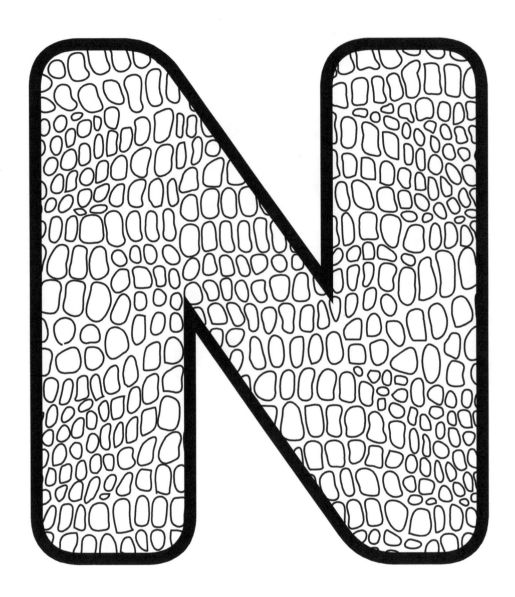

Newt

Newts can grow new legs and tails!

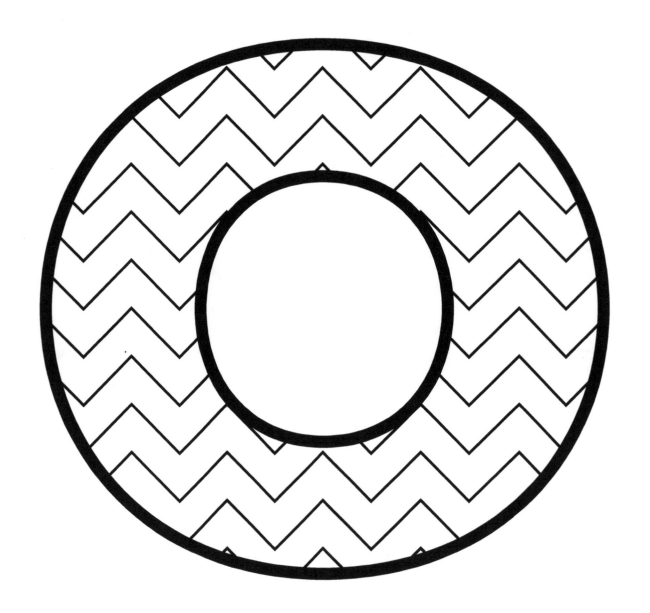

Octopus

An octopus can change color to blend in
with its surroundings.

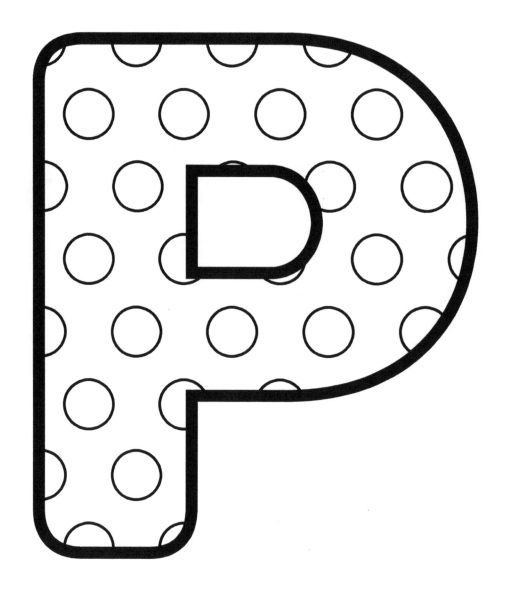

Panda

Pandas spend about 12 hours a day
eating bamboo.

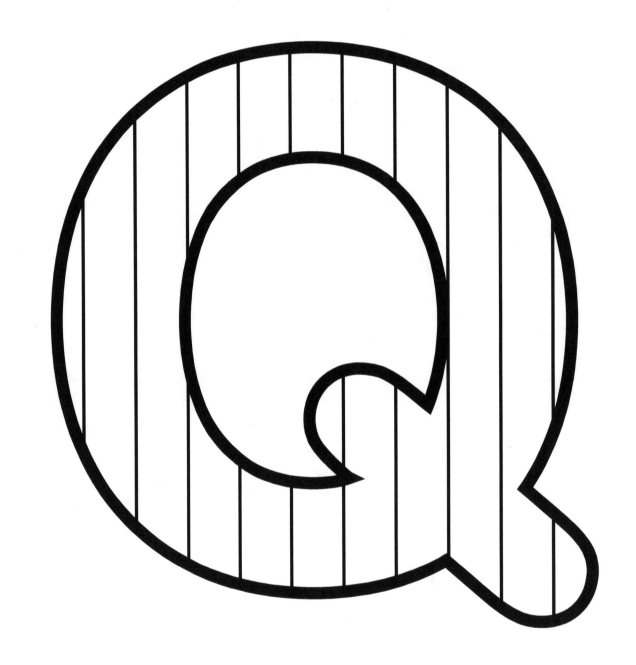

Quail

Quail are usually found in flocks called coveys.

Raccoon

Raccoons are nocturnal,
which means they're up all night!

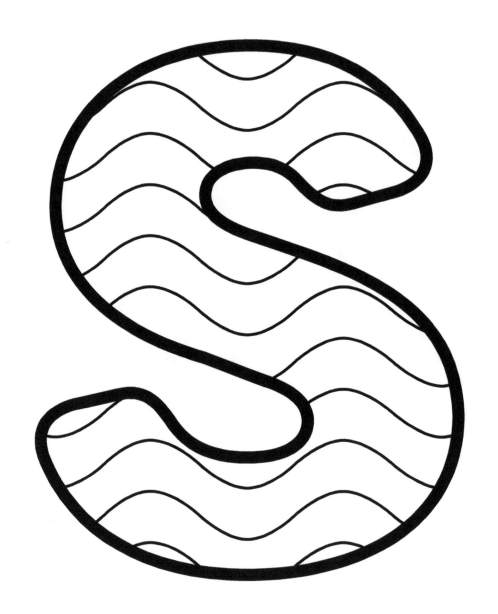

Seal

Seals have a thick layer of blubber that helps them stay warm in freezing cold water.

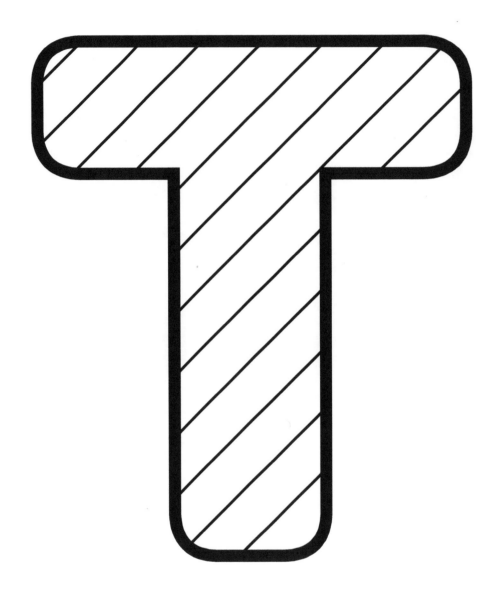

Turtle

Some turtles can weigh over 2,000 pounds!

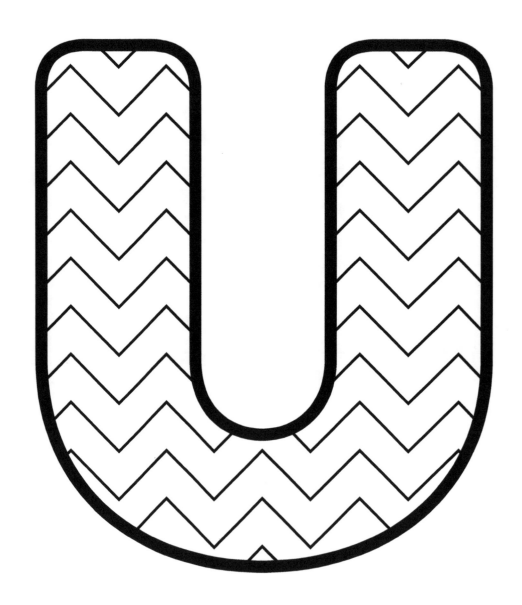

Urial

A urial is a type of wild sheep
that eats a lot of grass.

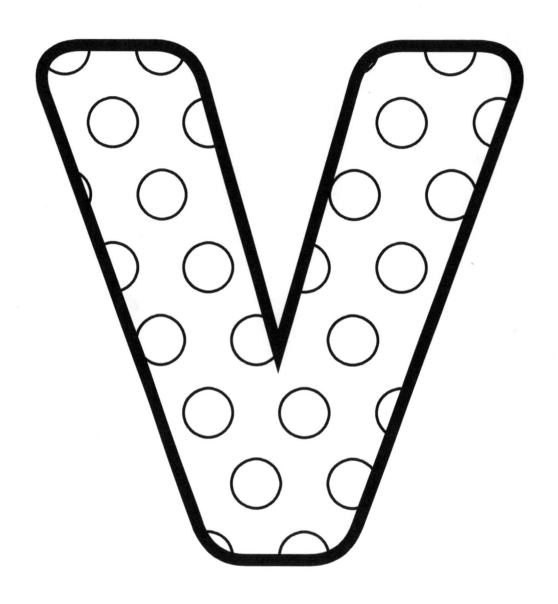

Vulture

Vultures have a very good sense of sight
and smell to help them find food.

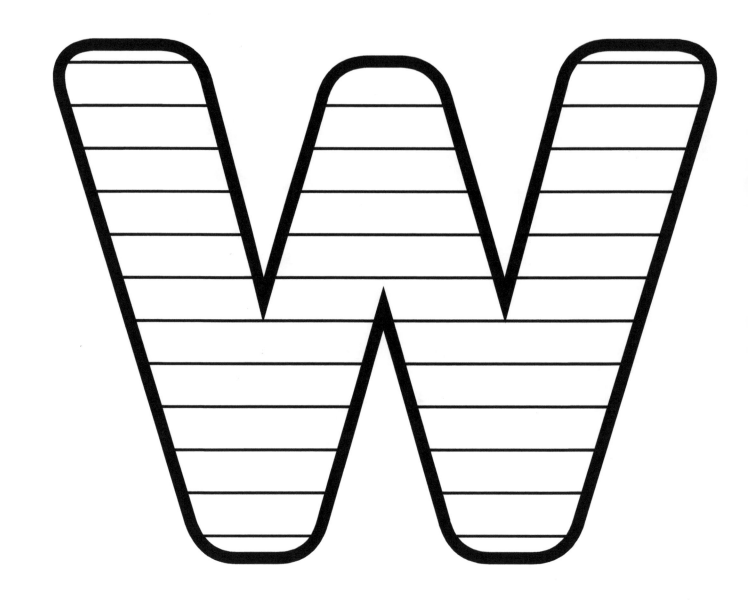

Whale

Whales talk to each other using clicks, whistles, and calls that sound like songs.

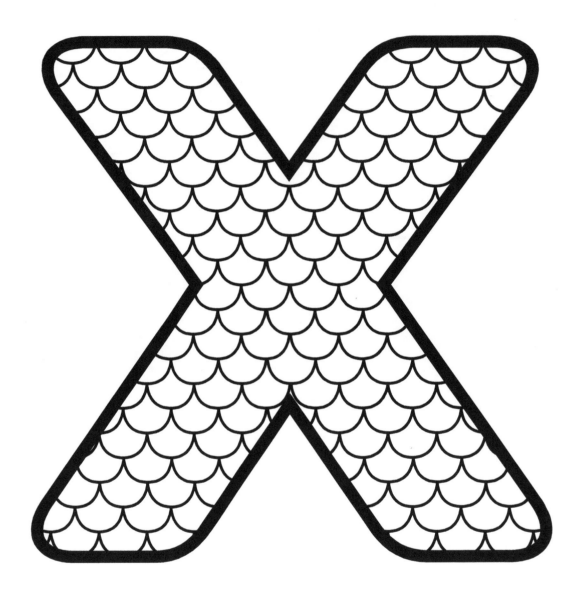

X-Ray Fish

An x-ray fish has see-through skin that lets you see its bones like an x-ray!

Yak

Yaks have long, thick hair
that keeps them warm.

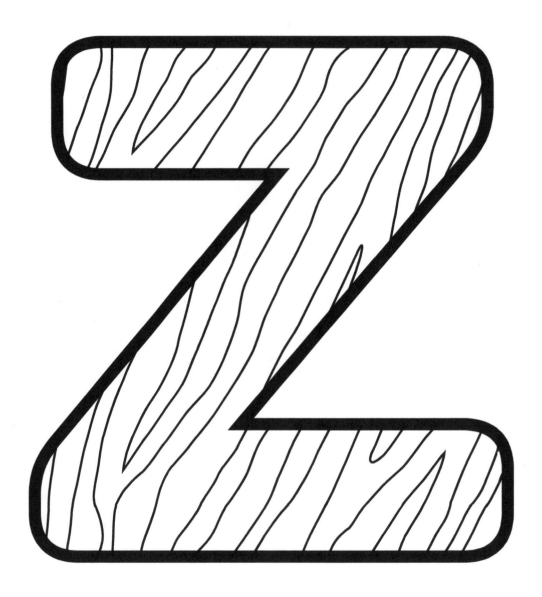

Zebra

Every zebra has its own special
stripe pattern.

About the Author

 **Rachael Smith** is the founder and curriculum designer of Literacy with the Littles (literacywiththelittles.com). Through her blog, she shares crafts and activities for parents and teachers that are designed to help little ones develop a love of learning. In 2010, she earned her bachelor's degree in early childhood education and began her teaching career. Rachael is a former first grade teacher turned stay-at-home mom. She is a wife and mother of four little ones. She enjoys crafting, traveling, spending time outdoors, and making memories with her family.

CPSIA information can be obtained
at www.ICGtesting.com
Printed in the USA
LVHW012341290919
632268LV00002BA/1/P